Mothers Day 2007
A gift for

Doodlie

From

Deersie

Thank you for
your lifelong example
of living a life of
love! I Love you.

A Mother's Love Is Precious

Illustrated by Tina Wenke

Sarah's Garden

Published by J. Countryman, a division of Thomas
Nelson, Inc, Nashville, Tennessee 37214.

Project editor—Terri Gibbs

Designed by Left Coast Design, Portland, Oregon.

ISBN: 1-4041-0096-2

www.thomasnelson.com
www.jcountryman.com

Printed and bound in the United States of America

A mother's love . . .

A mother's love
is humorous...

teaching us to laugh at ourselves,

to find joy in each day,

and to smile along

life's way.

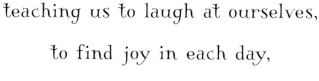

A mother's love
is generous...

showing us that what we have

is not nearly as important

as sharing what we have.

A mother's love
is one thing you
never outgrow.

Tina

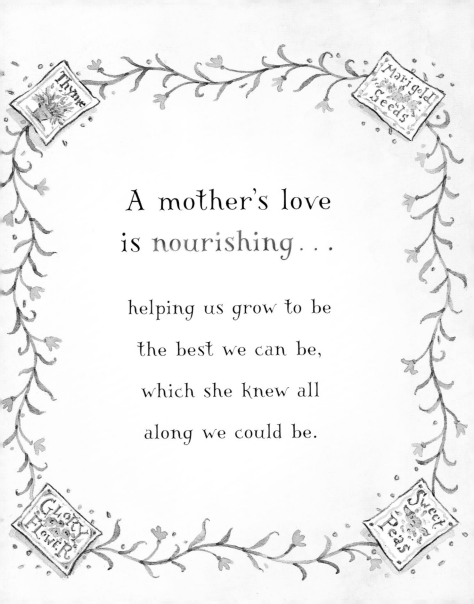

A mother's love
is nourishing...

helping us grow to be
the best we can be,
which she knew all
along we could be.

A mother's love
is positive...

reminding us time and again

that even on the most miserable

day there is something to

be happy about!

A mother's love is a long,
sweet prayer. . .

of whispered hopes
and quiet tears, winding
ever upward.

A mother's love
is determined . . .

never letting us settle for "good" or "fair" but insisting instead on "fabulous!"

A mother's love
is thoughtful...

taking time to say in so

many different ways,

"You are special to me!"

A mother's love
is priceless...

a gift without measure,

wrapped in memories

for life.

A mother's love
is patient...

knowing that children—

like flowers—grow best with

tender, loving care.

A mother's love
is one-of-a-kind.

There is nothing like it.

There is nothing to replace it.

A mother's love
is necessary...

everybody needs somebody to tell

them at least once a day~

"You're terrific!"

A mother's love
is awesome!

A mother's love
is amazing!

A mother's love
is wonderful!

A mother's love
is passionate!

A mother's love
is supportive.

A mother's love
is protective.

A mother's love
is limitless . . .

who can measure the hours

and days and months and years,

the hugs and kisses and prayers

and tears, the giving and

loving and caring?

A mother's love
builds a home...

the place she creates
for our family that makes
it uniquely our own.

A mother's love
reaches out and lifts
up even the child who
is hardest to love.

A mother's love is one
of the most beautiful
things in the world.

A mother's love
endures...

through diapers and dogs
and dodge balls and dates;
through tears and tantrums
and silliness and sighs.

A mother's love
is strong . . .

growing only deeper and

wider through heartbreak

or disappointment or

unexpected sorrow.

A mother's love
is a blessing...

a gift wrapped in wonder,
given by God.

A mother's love
is expansive...

giving us room to grow and learn

and do things on our own.

A mother's love
is joyful . . .

turning frowns to grins

and sighs to smiles

and sadness to gladness!

A mother's love is like

a summer garden...

lavish and lovely.

A mother's love
is precious...

perfectly suited,

and just the right size,

the best in the whole world

in each child's eyes.

A mother's love
is incredible!

Who else can turn

our doubts into dreams,

our fears into faith,

our pain into possibilities?

A mother's love is cause
for a celebration!
A parade!
A banquet!
A standing ovation!

A mother's love
is precious!